W9-DEN-357

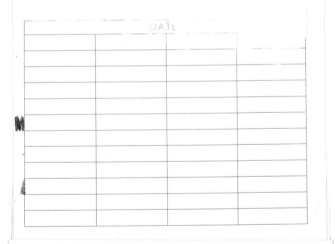

The T.F.H. Book of
CANARIES

Photographs: L. Arnall, 42 lower, 43. H. R. Axelrod,
36. Color Library International, 19, 73. P. Demko, 61.
H. V. Lacey: front and back covers, endpapers, 6, 8, 10,
11, 15, 20, 24 upper, 25, 26, 28, 30 upper, 31, 35, 37,
38, 45, 46, 47 upper, 53, 54, 56 lower, 57, 58, 60 lower,
62, 63, 65, 66, 67, 68, 69, 70, 72 lower, 74, 76 lower.
M. F. Roberts, 29 lower, 30 lower, 49, 51, 52 lower, 55,
72 upper. V. Serbin, 39. Courtesy of Vogelpark
Walsrode, 13, 27, 60 upper, 75, 76 upper, 77 upper.

ISBN 0-87666-819-8

Distributed in the U.S. by T.F.H. Publications, Inc., 211
West Sylvania Avenue, PO Box 427, Neptune, NJ 07753;
in England by T.F.H. (Gt. Britain) Ltd., 13 Nutley Lane,
Reigate, Surrey; in Canada to the pet trade by Rolf C.
Hagen Ltd., 3225 Sartelon Street, Montreal 382, Quebec;
in Canada to the book trade by H & L Pet Supplies, Inc., 27
Kingston Crescent, Kitchener, Ontario N28 2T6; in South-
east Asia by Y.W. Ong, 9 Lorong 36 Geylang, Singapore
14; in Australia and the South Pacific by Pet Imports Pty.
Ltd., P.O. Box 149, Brookvale 2100, N.S.W. Australia; in
South Africa by Valid Agencies, P.O. Box 51901, Randburg
2125 South Africa. Published by T.F.H. Publications, Inc.,
Ltd., the British Crown Colony of Hong Kong.

The T.F.H. Book of
CANARIES

Sue-Rhee Pasca

Young Glosters, all from the same nest.

Contents

Border canaries, clear male and variegated female.

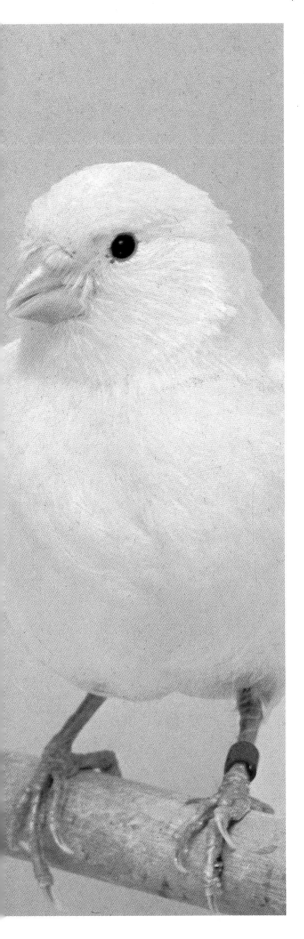

Introduction

The old-fashioned concept of the canary fancier as a kindly little old lady or a physically restricted invalid has, in recent years, gone to a long overdue demise. The modern canary keeper does not merely put a bird in a cage, feed it bird seed and wait for a burst of beautiful song. Rather, the modern fancier, although still in many cases the same little old lady or invalid, is a keen observer of avian life with a store of up-to-date knowledge plus a love of color and an ear for tonal beauty. The range of canary keepers too has expanded immeasurably. Canary breeding has become an activity for many adults of less than senior years whose interest has frequently matured into the founding of local clubs and their resulting competitions.

Many canary fanciers combine their hobby with a stereo hi-fi interest and record their pet's bursts of song for private and group entertainment. Canaries make excellent subjects for amateur photographers with picture sequences occasionally being entered in photography contests.

Home aviaries with a wide selection of different types of canaries form the nucleus of another growing area of hobby interest. Specialized breeding interests lead to an enlarged scope of social activities through club meetings and competitions.

As with other forms of pet keeping, the companionship of a canary often has therapeutic effects on individuals who keep them.

Scientific research has shown that canaries, in common with other forms of life, have their own method of "bird-to-bird communication." Little-known facts such as this frequently form the basis of a hobby interest that expands into other associated fields.

Thus it can be readily seen that the canary has assumed a new position of importance due, partially, to the greater knowledge and more fertile imagination of today's canary fancier. The canary hobbyist, whether he is destined to become a breeder and exhibitor or is content to keep a happy bird or two in a cage, requires a source of sound, accurate and nontechnical information covering the major aspects of the hobby. This, then, is the twofold purpose of this book—to fill the gap created by the need for more information in an accurate, specific but nontechnical form, and to illustrate to canary lovers some wider horizons for the enjoyment of this growing avocation. It cannot be emphasized too strongly, however, that a book cannot substitute for the years of practical experience which a pet-shop owner can offer to his customers and that such a relationship should be established from the beginning.

In our explorations of new worlds of interest, the longtime appeal of the canary as a source of color, beauty and companionship must not be overlooked. Cage birds have long been a source of solace to man. Parrots are known to have been kept by the ancient Romans; and starlings, nightingales, goldfinches and doves were mentioned as cage birds by many Latin writers.

Universally, the favorite cage bird for the past five centuries has been the canary. Selective breeding techniques during that period have led to the existence of most of the popular breeds of today. This emphasis on the domestication of canaries has proceeded so far that its natural environment is now the human home. Requiring a minimal investment of money, time and effort, canaries offer great advantages as pets to both the serious hobbyist and to those whose interest in them is more casual.

Inheritance in color canaries can be complex; here are a parent and two offspring.

History—Beauty with a Past

It was the song of the canary that captured the fancy of Europeans. The preeminent singer, the Roller, was developed by selective breeding.

In 1420, the Madeira Islands, off the west coast of Morocco, were added to the Portuguese empire by Portuguese men-o'-war and trading ships sailing under the aegis of Henry the Navigator. For at least a full century prior to that date, Madeira, as well as the Canary Islands and the Azores, was well known to the voyaging Genoese captains. Historical evidence indicates that large quantities of native birds, later destined to become known as "canaries," were captured during those years and shipped to the courts of Europe.

It is believed that Arabian ships cruising the Azores in the twelfth century were also familiar with the canary. Of older vintage are the accounts of Pliny the Elder (a Roman naturalist and contemporary of Christ) who left accounts of the avian life indigenous to the Canary Islands.

A hardy and alert songster, the original wild canary (*Serinus canarius*) spread through most of Europe. In England and Germany in particular, breeding became a most popular pastime. Whereas the Germans concentrated on developing exceptional singers, the English aimed at developing new strains featuring variations in appearance. The wild canary, an undistinguished green-hued little fellow measuring some four and a half inches in length, gave way with the passage of years to the soft-toned German Roller. The possibilities in breeding soon set fire to the imagination of many Europeans; and some unusual varieties featuring exceptional size, plumage, color and body shape were developed by the English, French, Belgians and Dutch.

Outstanding among these was the seventeenth-century Dutch Frill, an eight-inch giant sporting long, curly feathers on chest and shoulders. The English interest in varieties featuring short, brightly hued feathers resulted in the London Fancy and the Lizard. Subsequently, the English also developed the Norwich and the Yorkshire, both large birds of exceptional health and vitality.

Although major strides in breeding were made during these initial years of the canary's sojourn in Europe, the

11

Topography of
a canary:
1, crown
2, nape
3, neck
4, mantle
5, back
6, secondary flights
7, primary flights
8, tail
9, forehead
10, beak
11, throat
12, shoulders
13, breast
14, wing coverts
15, abdomen
16, thigh
17, leg
18, toe

twentieth century has also seen new directions opened to canary fanciers. The white canary, another color variant, was developed after the turn of the century. More recently, breeders have crossed the canary with the Hooded Siskin.

Perhaps in scientific breeding more than in any other area does the real future of canary keeping lie. Here is a field in which considerable progress in variation is still possible and in which a large proportion of hobbyist interest has been manifested. Combined with the modern knowledge of genetics and nutrition, many canary fanciers see this as tomorrow's horizon for canary keeping.

The breeds of type canaries are characterized by differences in feathering, body shape, and posture. The Northern Dutch Frill above is considerably different in build from the Norwich below.

Description and Characteristics

The accompanying illustration shows some basic terms used in describing perching birds of the order Passeriformes, to which the canary belongs. It might appear that birds as different as the Dutch Frill and the Crested canaries might belong to different species. However, these differences are in color and in feather arrangement, not in the basic structure of the bird.

FEATHERS

During the daytime, when the bird is feeling well, the feathers will be held close to the body giving the bird a sleek, trim appearance. If the room temperature drops, you will notice that the bird will fluff its feathers, giving the appearance of a soft ball much like the chickadees and sparrows that live outside during the cold winter months. This type of fluffing of the feathers gives a maximum of dead air space and hence considerable insulating value. You will also notice when the bird is asleep that the feathers are fluffed for the same purpose—so that it will be cozy and warm. If the bird does not feel well, the feathers will be fluffed abnormally during the daytime to counteract the feeling of chill which comes along with illness.

During the summer on very hot days you will notice another type of feather response. In this case the bird tends to keep the feathers very sleek or compressed, the wings are held away from the body, and the beak is held open. When this happens the bird should be placed in a cooler place and given cool water for bathing. By now you have observed your canary enough to know that when it sleeps it not only fluffs its feathers but also tucks its head back into the feathers on its back.

BODY TEMPERATURE

The normal body temperature of your canary is very high—about 109 degrees Fahrenheit as compared to your own normal temperature of about 98.6 degrees Fahrenheit. The high body temperature combined with a high rate of metabolism in your bird means that its system uses up food rapidly, and in consequence it must eat frequently throughout the day. It is for this reason that your bird is not able to survive long without food and therefore should have food available in its cups at all times. You will notice that as the sun goes down, your bird will go to the food cups and fill its crop with seeds to last through the night.

BREATHING

Your bird does not have pores in its skin to regulate body temperature by perspiring as we do, but instead it cools itself by breathing with its mouth open; by holding its feathers in such a way that air can penetrate to the skin surface or by compressing them tightly to reduce the dead air spaces; and by bathing in or drinking cool water. The canary has a much more extensive breathing apparatus than we have. When your bird inhales air it passes through the lungs and then into a system of air sacs which even extend into hollow spaces in some of the bones. In this respect, your bird's respiratory system acts somewhat like the cooling system of an air-cooled motor.

Speaking of breathing, your canary inhales about 100 times a minute as compared to only twelve times a minute for humans.

HEART RATE

While human hearts beat at a rate of about seventy to eighty beats per minute, your canary's heart beats at the rate of 800 to 1,000 times per minute when it is standing quietly. This will explain why you can feel a delicate vibration like that of a small motor when you hold your canary gently in your hand.

PREENING

Frequently your canary will sort through its feathers with its beak—a process called preening. Occasionally you may notice that your bird will reach back into the feathers just above the point of attachment of the long tail feathers and do something with its beak at that point. Actually, the bird is squeezing a small oil gland (uropygial gland) to get a supply of a fatty material which it then rubs on its feathers, feet and beak to keep the surfaces protected with a layer of oil. Periodically you will see your bird sorting its feathers and actually pulling feathers through the beak. Some of this sorting is done after the bird flies around and settles back on its perch and in this case, it is merely done to rearrange feathers which have gotten slightly out of place during the more vigorous movements of flight.

If your bird is not feeling well, you will notice that the preening or oiling of the feathers is not carried out regularly and the feathers will take on a dull, dry look.

One of the best signs that your bird is feeling better after an illness is that it will begin to preen again, just as people enjoy "dolling up" after recovery from sickness.

Young Border, variegated.

EATING AND DIGESTION

Now let's talk a little about how your canary eats and digests its food. After your bird has been at the food cups for a while, you will notice an accumulation of seed husks in or around the cup. Your canary has no teeth so it has no way of chewing the seeds in its mouth. Instead it discards the husk and swallows the seed whole. The seed passes down the throat into a long tube called the esophagus. At one point the esophagus is a little larger and stretches readily, and here the seeds that are eaten accumulate much like food materials accumulate for a while in our own stomachs. This region where the seeds pause at first is called the crop. Actually the canary's crop is not as well developed as the crop of the chicken but is merely a place in the esophagus which expands temporarily for the purpose of storing food. The food then passes into the glandular stomach, or proventriculus, where there is considerable moistening of the food materials and digestive enzymes commence to work.

Next the softened food which has been mixed with digestive enzymes passes into the muscular stomach, or gizzard. The gizzard contains gravel which the bird has eaten and stored for the purpose of helping to grind up the food. From the gizzard the food, now in finely ground form, passes into the small intestine where further digestive processes and absorption of the nutrients occur. Besides the enzymes which help to digest the food and which come from the body, there are other enzymes produced by the action of helpful bacteria which live in the intestinal tract. These bacteria even help in the synthesis of certain vitamins and other nutrients which the bird needs. Finally, the waste materials pass further down the intestinal tract, turning from light green in color to a grayish brown or black as they approach the lower end of the intestinal tract.

The last small section of the intestinal tract near the vent is called the cloaca. The kidney wastes are also voided into the cloaca, where they mix with the intestinal residues and are passed out through the vent as typical canary droppings. The urine of the canary is a white semi-solid mass, which is the white portion you will observe in your bird's droppings.

There will be some variation in consistency and appearance of the droppings from day to day depending upon the type of food eaten and the amount of water consumed. If, however, there is a marked change in the appearance of the droppings, check with your veterinarian.

LIFE SPAN

With good food and care your canary should sing lustily and live happily in your home for many years. It is of in-

Commercially available seed mixes for canaries have canary and rape seeds as their main ingredients.

Facing page: The light-colored seeds in the food dish are canary seed; the dark ones are rape.

terest to note, however, that female canaries, owing to the loss of vitality during the breeding season, may not live more than five or six years. Yet there are some canaries, apparently males, which have been known to reach the ripe old age of sixteen years. One expert reports knowing of one that was twenty years old and still active.

THE CANARY SONG

A young male canary gradually learns to sing, and by the time he is about six months old he should be in full song. Only the male birds engage in full singing, although occasionally a female bird may come forth with a few warbling notes. Among breeders and fanciers, birds are often bred for a particular type of singing. For example, you may hear someone speak of a chopper, a roller or a singer, depending upon the specialized type of vocalization. At any rate, it is not necessary to know what type of song your pet canary sings in order to enjoy its beauty.

If you play the piano, you may be interested to know that most of the higher-pitched bird songs in nature are in the octave just above the piano keyboard. Your bird's song is higher than the highest soprano voice and also in a range higher than the violin, flute or piccolo. The more carefully you listen to your canary's song, the more notes you will detect, but some of the notes are sung so rapidly that they can't be distinguished by the human ear. It has been shown, through scientific studies at a leading university, that some of the small song birds average sixteen different notes per second while singing. Notes lasting only 0.002 seconds in duration have been recorded.

There are certain times of the year when your canary will sing more lustily. The months from October to March, for example, are usually the best singing months. Your pet bird may even cease singing entirely during the molting period which occurs during the hotter months of the year.

Above: A vegetable food will contain, besides seeds, bits of dried greens and other vegetables. Below: Song food includes ingredients that are believed to stimulate singing.

Border canary, clear yellow in color, buff in texture.

Scotch Fancy, one of the "posture " or "position" breeds.

Many of the canaries available today still show the yellow and brownish green of their wild ancestors.

Selecting the Canary

THE FIRST STEP

The best way to get started in canary keeping is to buy your first canary. The old Chinese maxim which states that "the thousand-mile journey begins with the first step" is quite appropriate here. Buy your first canary. Become familiar with the intricacies of the canary hobby through acquiring a little practical experience. Then, and only then, decide how far to go into the hobby and on what aspect to concentrate.

The first step in the initial purchase is, usually, to drop around to a number of stores and observe the various canaries. Talk to the owner or manager and get his opinion. Then, finally, decide to buy from a clean, well-run establishment whose knowledgeable personnel have created a favorable impression.

The primary thing to expect from the seller is a written guarantee in respect to the bird's singing ability. Not infrequently, the selected bird has only recently arrived and is not yet acclimated to the new surroundings. However, once the bird is in your home it can be expected to start singing within a week or two.

It is well to remember that it is the male canary who sings. Since, to the amateur, most young canaries look alike, particularly before the first molt, the ability to sing is frequently used to determine the sex of the bird. The female also makes an excellent pet because of her pleasant voice and her ready adaptability to training, but because females do not sing, their prices are usually much lower. The price of a male is determined both by his type and the quality of his song.

The main step after the decision to buy, therefore, is to obtain a written guarantee from the dealer stating that it is a male and will sing.

The next factors to consider are the general health of the bird; the cage and cage furnishings; and the type of bird to choose. Here is a brief checklist of signs of health and disease to be closely watched for in the prospective pet:

A healthy canary is a lively canary. It is active in the cage and moves in an alert manner.

When seeking a pet canary, many people look for a completely yellow bird.

Even if the canary is not singing, it will at least be calling and chirping. If the canary is healthy, its appearance will be clean and lithe.

A sick bird is quiet and listless. Its feathers are puffed up and it sits on the perch almost continuously.

A canary with a cold shivers and sneezes. There is a slight watery discharge, and the droppings are white and watery.

If the canary has sore eyes, it may rub its head against the sides of the perch or the cage bars. The eyes will be inflamed and reddish.

Observe the general cleanliness of the installation where you intend to make your purchase and, in particular, the cleanliness of the prospective pet's cage.

CANARY BREEDS

Here is a checklist of some of the kinds of canaries available today. Many other varieties, bred in the past, declined because of lack of popularity. Others were not hardy enough to survive. Since, at this early stage, the basic idea is to make your first purchase and start to get practical experience, it would probably be best to select one of the more readily available kinds.

Commercial Canary: Many of the more exotic breeds have died out simply because the general public was quite satisfied with the "commercial" canaries sold in most pet stores. The song of these birds is, in many cases, far superior to the song of the more exotic breeds which were originally bred for type or color rather than for voice.

Above: The song of a canary depends in part on how it is delivered. The open beak means a brighter, louder, and sometimes harsher song, while the soft-singing Roller keeps its beak closed. Below: The plumage of this canary shows the ability to produce red pigment, inherited from the Hooded Siskin.

The song of the standard canary is bright and cheerful, with crisp, bell tones blended with the notes common to the Roller canary. If a softer, Roller-type song is preferred, it will be found that in any group of singers there is at least one bird with a softer tone. The clerk or manager should be consulted on this choice and his advice followed.

The size of the "commercials" is four or five inches. The color of the plumage is either bright yellow, yellow, yellow and green, or an occasional all-green singer who is a throwback to the first wild birds.

Roller: Most other varieties are bred for color or form; the Roller canary has been bred for his soft, distinctive voice. The clear, thrilling quality of a Roller's song leaves a canary lover enchanted. Just like a good opera singer, a champion Roller has a naturally beautiful voice, but it needs training and practice to use it to best effect. Young birds get this training by listening to, and imitating, adult singers called "tutors." Nowadays, of course, the songs, or "tours," of a champion Roller can be recorded, and the recording may then be used to train young singers. Remember, Rollers learn by listening to an accomplished singer. If you keep young Rollers where they can hear other birds, they are likely to pick up undesirable though possibly interesting songs.

Before buying or breeding these birds make sure you remember they are soft-singing birds, whose song is much different from the bright, varied song so much in demand. If you do like this soft song, one interesting point about Rollers is that they can be trained to sing at night when their gentle voices seem particularly appropriate.

Chopper: Like the Roller, the Chopper is distinctive not so much for his color or shape as for his type of song. Where a Roller sings with his mouth closed, or slightly open, a Chopper opens and closes his bill during song. This is because he combines chirps, notes, trills and warbles into a varied song. The song of the Warbler is usually low and sweet while that of the Chopper more broken up and with many of the notes almost clarion-like.

American Singer: Widely favored at present, this breed was achieved principally by crossing Rollers with Borders, in an attempt to increase the volume of the Roller song while still preserving its character.

Red-factor: For many years, canary fanciers tried to develop a strain of red canaries. Many different wild birds with red plumage were mated with canaries but without success. Then approximately fifty years ago, the German breeder, Dr. Hans Duncker, suggested that a small South American bird, the Hooded Siskin, would mate with the canary.

Since that time, breeders have tried many combinations of these birds. However, it is only within the last decades that the strain has been perfected. These handsome newcomers can be found in all shades from very light orange, to copper, to a deep orange-red that is almost a pure red.

In addition to inheriting the handsome colors of their fathers, the Hooded Siskins, Red-factor canaries also have the clear, liquid voice of their canary mothers. Because of the lovely song and striking appearance of these beautiful birds, they are usually more expensive than the other varieties.

Color Canaries: In addition to the Red-factors, other color varieties are popular nowadays. Many mutations have occurred, so that factors for white, brown, agate, pastel, ino and satinet—and their combinations—make color breeding a fascinating part of the canary fancy.

Lizard: Lizard canaries are one of the oldest types still bred. Profitable breeding of Lizard canaries requires great care and is not recommended to the beginner. One interesting point about this variety is that they are in their best plumage during their first year. After that time, the spangles which give the Lizard its distinctive appearance fade and become insignificant.

Border: These canaries are quite popular among type breeders of today. Borders are large birds and are very hardy and prolific. They are, therefore, good birds for the newcomer to try breeding. They are called Borders because they were first bred in the counties along the border between England and Scotland.

Norwich: Robust and heavier birds, Norwich canaries are not quite as free breeders as are the Borders. They probably originated in the city of Norwich, England. This breed also provided the body type sought in the development of Crested canaries.

Yorkshire: Sometimes called the "gentleman" of the canary world because of its graceful, slim body and good posture, the Yorkshire was first developed about a hundred years ago and has been popular ever since. At one time, it was said that a good Yorkshire could pass through a wedding ring. The Yorkshires of today are not quite so slim. They are hardy birds, good for newcomers to the hobby.

Gloster: One of the newer breeds, the Glosters were first recognized in the 1930s. They are one of the smallest of the popular varieties of canary and have stout bodies. Some of them are crested (coronas), and some are plain-headed (consorts).

Lancashire: Unfortunately, this great bird has been slowly disappearing until now it is scarce even in its native

Above: Yorkshires, five weeks old. Below: The inheritance of this canary involves both the red and the crested factors.

Border canary. The buff feathering is apparent here.

Canaries are frequently crossed with other related
bird species, such as the European Goldfinch and
the Linnet—which are the parents of this hybrid.

England. The Lancashire is the giant of canaries; it is not only the largest but is also one of the oldest breeds. There are two kinds: one with a plain head and one with a crest, or coppy. The crest is distinctive because it covers only the front half of the head, suggesting that the Lancashire is wearing a cap.

Frills: Up to eight inches long, Frills were probably first bred in Holland. They are different from all the other types of canary in that they have long, curly feathers that appear to grow inside out. Although excitable parents, they are not too hard to breed and constitute a good choice for the beginner who wishes to raise canaries that are really distinctive. Many male Frills are excellent singers.

Belgian and Scotch Fancies: Unusual posture is the keynote of these birds. Featuring long, thin bodies with shallow chests and long necks and tail feathers, they perch with their heads stuck forward from their bodies, or drooping down, so that they form a half circle. Although an interesting type, these birds have never been as popular as some of the others, probably because people are unaccustomed to their unusual shape. They are also called Slims.

The difference in feather length between the yellow Parisian Frill and the darker Northern Dutch Frill is difficult to distinguish in these photographs.

The heavy-bodied Norwich is also one of the largest canary breeds.

Above: While a single bird might be kept permanently in a cage this small, the bird would be able to exercise more in a cage only a little larger. Below: In most situations, the widely popular tube drinker is the best device to supply water to canaries in a cage.

Housing and Acclimating

At this early stage of the hobby, it is jumping the gun to go to such extremes as selecting an elaborate cage to blend in with the decor of the home. There are a great many kinds of cages available in many shapes and many colors. These vary from a foot or so square to two or three feet in length. The size and the degree of fashion is limited only by the amount of money one wishes to invest. It is best to be guided by the advice of the pet-store personnel.

The amount of money required to purchase bird, cage, cage furnishings and food is minimal. Here, too, the pet dealer can save the hobbyist a considerable amount of time by giving proper and knowledgeable advice. Basically, the dealer will say that you need: a cage equipped with perches, three or four food cups, bird gravel, cuttlebone, bird seed and diet supplements.

CAGE FURNISHINGS

Your new pet needs several round or oval-shaped soft-wood perches in its cage. These should be of slightly different size so its feet don't get tired from always gripping in the same position. You may even wish to provide the canary with a flat perch an inch or more wide so that it may sometimes sit without having to cling at all.

Any new cage you purchase will be fitted with the necessary perches. Don't make the mistake of adding more perches so that the bird will have to fly through an obstacle course. Leave it a clear flyway so that it can get the necessary exercise. Also, check the perches periodically to make sure they are not loose and cannot turn when the canary alights.

The cage should have one cup for food and another for water. One or two treat cups, fitted to the wires of the cage, should also be provided. These are for such treats and supplementary foods as song food, conditioning food and fresh greens. A cuttlebone should be hung close to a perch and changed regularly. This not only keeps the beak in condition, but it also adds calcium to the diet. The floor of the cage should be covered with a thin layer of bird gravel. Gravel paper can also be used.

Any new cage will be painted or finished with materials that cannot harm your bird. If you decide to repaint an old cage, or alter the color of a new one, do not use a paint that has lead in it. Lead is poisonous to birds just as it is to humans. It is wise to avoid any oil paint. Use the latex types. Don't put your pet back into a freshly painted cage too soon. Also, it is best to keep your canary in a room well away from the odor of fresh paint whenever your home is being redecorated.

TOYS

Bird toys such as a swing, a ladder or a bell can be placed in your canary's cage so that your pet will not become bored. Remember, though, not to clutter your bird's cage, or it will not have room to exercise its wings.

ACCLIMATING THE CANARY

Although canaries are highly domesticated, they are still capable of feeling ill at ease for the first few days in new surroundings. The pet has been subject to several changes in environment over a relatively short time and, therefore, requires a certain period in which to adjust. Until the canary shows signs of adjusting, do not expect it to sing. Permit the pet some privacy and see that it is well fed and warm.

When you first get the canary home, let it enter the cage by itself. Put the opened traveling box up to the open door of the cage and leave it there until the bird hops into the cage. If it has not gone into the cage voluntarily within an hour or so, pick it up gently and put it into the cage. The bird must be picked up *gently*. Hold it from on top so that your hand covers the wings but leaves the feet free to move. Never grab a bird by the legs or tail or squeeze it to prevent struggling.

After your canary becomes accustomed to the new surroundings, it will greet you and your friends with a cheery song. As with humans, canaries like sunshine and a light room, but they cannot stand hot summer sun. Make sure that no drafts reach the cage because chills are bad for birds and endanger their health. The cage should be covered from sunset to sunrise, particularly if strong artificial light is present. With insufficient sleep, the bird's health and singing ability can be adversely affected.

Above: In assessing the quality of Crested and Crestbred canaries, the head receives as much attention as the rest of the body. Below: Canaries brought into a new environment should be left unbothered for a few days.

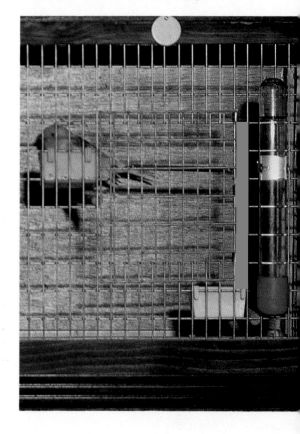

Facing page: Canaries should have perches of a size that allows the claws on the longest toes to come into contact with the wood.

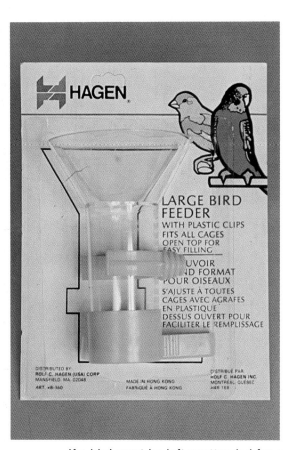

LARGE BIRD
FEEDER
WITH PLASTIC CLIPS
FITS ALL CAGES
OPEN TOP FOR
EASY FILLING

If a bird must be left unattended for a
couple of days, feeders like the one
shown above will hold an ample supply.

Facing page: The seed dish shown here
will hold enough seed for only a day
or two at most.

Feeding the Canary

The canary fancier who decides to enlarge the scope of his hobby will, eventually, come to realize the immense importance of proper diet. The foundations of proper nutrition, however, are basically the same for both the casual pet and the more specialized breeding varieties.

In general, the canary requires a balanced diet consisting, as does the human diet, of protein, carbohydrates, fats, vitamins and minerals. The only difference between the balanced diet you feed your family and the balanced diet you feed your pet is the source of the various nutrients.

The canary's meals should consist mainly of a daily seed mixture, supplementary foods and treat foods, cuttlebone, grit and plenty of fresh water. The average canary weighs approximately two-thirds of an ounce and consumes about one-eighth ounce, or about one teaspoonful, of food per day. While this amount of food is very small by our own eating standards, it nevertheless represents considerable food when one looks at the weight of the canary. In other words, your canary eats an amount of food equal to about one-fifth of its body weight every day. This would compare to a 150-pound man eating thirty pounds of food a day! Your canary's higher rate of metabolism and higher temperature require that it eat more. This means that you must take special pains to make sure that your bird has before it at all times a sufficient quantity of food. Special attention should be given to make certain that the food cups actually contain food and not merely discarded seed husks. Every year, pet birds starve to death with their seed cups filled with husks, because the owners, on glancing quickly at the cups, assumed that there was plenty of food left. Because of their high rate of metabolism, canaries are not able to fast for any length of time and will die within twenty-four or forty-eight hours if food and water are not available.

CHIEF FOOD

A canary's chief food is seed. The daily seed mixture consists of seeds grown specifically for canaries and is known simply as canary mix. Canary seed is a long, narrow tan seed, pointed at each end. Mixed with the canary seed are rape seeds, a very nourishing seed that canaries like, and an assortment of other seeds in small amounts that give the bird different flavors and extra food values.

Give the canary fresh seed every day. It likes its food clean, fresh and sweet. Be sure that there is always seed in the cup—and that it *is* seed! Canaries husk the seeds before eating them, frequently dropping the husks back into the seed cup. This may give the cup the appearance of being full when it contains nothing of nutritive value. Blow gently on the mixture; the husks, which are lighter in weight, will blow away, leaving the seed.

SUPPLEMENTARY FOODS

Canary lovers have discovered that their pets appreciate and thrive on supplementary foods that help build resistance against sickness. Certain wild seeds are so appetizing that finding them in their cages from time to time acts as a signal for the canaries to start a song concert. The popular brands of bird foods provide such supplementary treats in the form of conditioning foods, song foods and molting foods.

Breeders have also discovered that eggs have value for canaries. A convenient way to provide the benefits of fresh egg is the commercially prepared egg-biscuit food that can be fed in conjunction with other supplementary foods. All of the above can be given in the special treat cups previously described.

TREATS

Most canaries also relish certain treats such as biscuits or charms that are actually a mixture of different seeds cooked with honey. Other treats come in the form of little plastic cups which fit right on the cage, in which greens are grown or millet seeds are provided. Bird-seed bells or millet sprays can also serve as treats. Fresh greens and fruits should be given; special care must be taken to make sure that all insecticides or other chemicals have been carefully washed from them. The benefits of many varieties of greens and fruits can be furnished in commercial mixtures that supply these products and fruits in dehydrated form, sometimes mixed with seeds.

In case you have never fed a canary before, here is a word of warning about treats. The items listed in the preceding paragraph are treats appropriate for a canary. Delicacies such as cake from your table are entirely unsuitable. If your pet becomes fat and listless, it will stop singing. The best singers are the birds fed on proper canary food with the supplementary foods that are real "treats" for them.

Greens, available in a convenient dry form, are a beneficial part of a canary diet.

Facing page: Border male, variegated.

CUTTLEBONE

Minerals and salts round out the canary's diet. It can get these from a piece of cuttlebone, which is the internal calcareous shell of the cuttlefish. A piece of this bone should hang in the cage at all times, soft side in. By picking at it, the bird will keep its bill sharp, and the calcium in the cuttlebone will keep its bones strong and its beak hard. You will have to replace the cuttlebone about once a month.

WATER

Canaries love fresh water and they drink quite a bit. Be sure your pet is *never* left without plenty of fresh water. During the summer months it is best to give fresh water twice a day. Of course, your pet will want to drink from a clean cup. Wash it daily so that it remains as clean as your own china.

BIRD GRAVEL

A little further on, you will learn about the use of bird gravel, or grit, as a part of good housekeeping. It also plays a part in feeding. Birds have no teeth; food is swallowed and stored in the crop. From there it enters the gizzard where the food is thoroughly ground up so that its nutriments can be utilized. In order for the gizzard to do its work efficiently, the canary *must* eat a little gravel. Keep an ample supply on the bottom of the cage where the bird can scratch around and pick up what it needs.

1

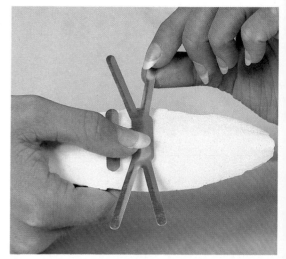

2

The cuttlebone available in pet shops (1) is the processed internal shell of a squid. The thin metal holder should be held against the harder side (2) and bent around (3).

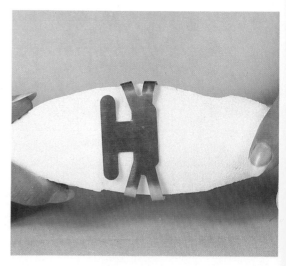

3

Buff Yorkshire, variegated.

Gold Lizard, broken capped.

Canary Housekeeping

Above: If gravel is not used to cover the floor of the cage, it should be supplied in a small dish. Below: Eating a treat is not only nutritious, it also provides activity.

CAGE UPKEEP

Since cleanliness and sanitation are the fundamental preventives of disease, it is essential that the installation of a new pet in your home be accompanied with a program of proper canary housekeeping.

The program is an easy one, requiring only a few moments of routine effort. Following are some of the basic techniques recommended by authorities on canary keeping.

Every other day the bottom of the cage should be cleaned out and a fresh layer of gravel supplied. Paper in the floor absorbs the liquid from the droppings and makes cleaning easier.

Clean the perches every time you clean the cage bottom. Do not wash them—the dampness can result in rheumatism—but scrape them with wire perch-scrapers available in pet shops.

Once a week, clean the cage thoroughly. Wash the walls and bars with a damp cloth or scrub them with soapy water. Then spray the cage with a mild disinfectant to keep away mites and other pests. Of course, during this kind of cleaning, you should put your pet in a spare cage. Make sure that the regular cage is thoroughly dry after washing before returning the bird to it.

BATHS

Your canary will do much to keep itself clean. It will spend hours preening its feathers to keep them clean and well arranged. As part of its plumage-care program, see that your pet gets regular baths. During the summer, allow your canary the health-giving fun of a clean bath three or four times a week, if not every day. During the winter, about once a week is enough, but make sure that the room is warm.

You can buy a little bird bath that attaches to the side of the cage, or you can put some lukewarm water (about half an inch) in a shallow bowl on the bottom of the cage. Your pet will probably want to splash about and shake itself so much that it will leave a messy bath just like a frisky youngster. Then you will have to clean and dry the cage—never keep a canary in a damp cage. If your bird is hesitant about bathing, splash a little water on it when you set out the bath or, even better, buy a bath with a fine mist spray.

Nibbling at buds points up a canary's taste for greens.

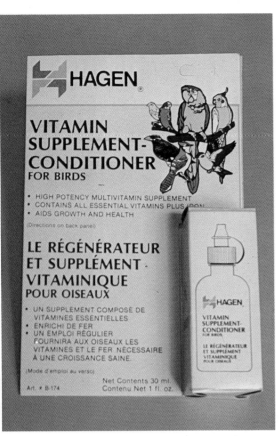

Above: Many birdkeepers supplement the diet of their canaries regularly with a vitamin complex. Below: Nutritive value aside, the tonic block, like the cuttlebone, also serves to keep a bird's beak in trim.

CARE—THE BEST PREVENTIVE

Canaries are hardy birds which have lived so long in human society that man's dwelling has become their natural environment. If your canary is properly cared for, it will live a happy, contented life, filling your home with its cheery song. Your pet's resistance to disease *always* goes hand in hand with good care and proper feeding. The best way to avoid sickness in the canary is always to follow the rules for a canary's diet outlined in a preceding section.

Care is just as important as proper diet. This involves regular housecleaning, including the cleaning of water and food cups, the bottom of the cage, perches and the cage itself. Canaries should be kept out of drafts and should never be left out in the bright sun.

A heartbreaking accident may occur if your canary escapes from its cage, unless you take care to prevent it. Mirrors are dangerous because a bird may fly directly into them. Household appliances can be threats to your pet's safety. Unscreened windows and outside doors should always be kept closed if there is any chance of your pet's escaping from its cage.

AILMENTS

Here follows a summary of some of the most frequently encountered ailments of the canary, their symptoms and treatment. If your pet becomes ill, recovery will be more rapid if you provide the proper treatment. Remember, however, that a veterinarian should be consulted if your canary doesn't show improvement in a day or two.

Colds: *Symptoms*: Looks puffed up, listless. Bird shivers and occasionally sneezes. Slight watery discharge from the nostrils. Droppings white and watery. *Treatment*: Keep the bird warm and quiet, day and night. If it stays on the cage bottom, food and water cups should be placed beside it. Some of the softer supplementary foods such as conditioning food or egg biscuit should be moistened with a commercially prepared liquid tonic, available at most pet shops.

Asthma: This can be caused by drafts and bad ventilation. The most common cause is a dirty cage causing the bird to breathe dust, which inflames the respiratory organs.

Symptoms: Breathing laborious, gasping for air. Each breath may be accompanied by wheezing or squeaking. *Treatment*: Same as for colds.

Constipation: *Symptoms*: Infrequent and hard droppings. The bird appears unable to evacuate without jerky movement and with apparent discomfort. General listlessness and lack of appetite. *Treatment*: Add more greens to the diet. As an immediate measure, provide fresh greens like watercress. As a more permanent measure, furnish your pet with a regular supply of live, growing greens that come in treat cups. These cups can be obtained at most pet shops. Allow more exercise.

Diarrhea: *Symptoms*: Loose droppings with a large portion of white matter. Vent feathers slightly wet at first, and then more and more soiled. The canary will be inactive and sit with ruffled-up feathers. *Treatment*: Withhold green foods for a few days; feed only seed. Some bird experts recommend fresh buttermilk or yoghurt mixed in the drinking water during intestinal troubles.

Baldness: Sometimes baldness may be caused by mites. Other causes are skin trouble or a feather-picking habit by another bird in the same cage. High temperature is another likely cause. The cage may be too near a radiator or a stove. *Treatment*: Use one of the many good ointments on the market if you are sure that mites or too high a temperature is *not* the cause. If high temperature is causing loss of feathers, remove the canary at once to a more moderate temperature. The solution to feather-picking is obvious. Separate your canaries. Mites can be exterminated by the methods listed later.

Sore eyes: Unless sore eyes are obviously caused by an injury, they should be treated as an infectious disease. Your pet may start rubbing the sides of its head against its perch or against its cage. Eyelids and eyes become inflamed and reddish. *Treatment*: Buy some eye solution of the same strength your druggist would sell for human use. Wash your pet's eyes with this solution.

Sore feet: The main cause is a dirty cage. Other causes are rough or dirty perches. Prevention is the answer here—provide good care and treatment will not be needed. If it is, there are ointments available at your pet shop. Wash your pet's feet every day in warm water and apply the ointment. Don't try to pick off scales or rough pieces of skin—this is painful for the bird

Broken bones: Dislocation of toe joints, broken legs or other injuries are frequently caused when birds become frightened and panic. When they dash about their cages in fright, they are likely to catch their feet in a crack or crevice. Again, preventive action is very important. Don't

Above: Norwich canary with "lumps" caused by ingrowing feathers. Below: In the case of this canary, the cause of the baldness could not be determined.

Above: Mite infestation of the foot. Below: The bands used to identify birds may be implicated in conditions such as the dry gangrene shown here.

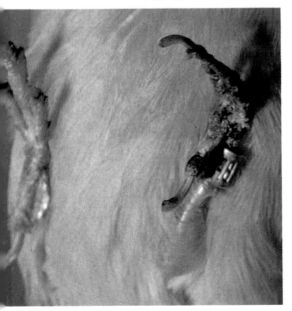

allow conditions that can frighten your pet to arise. Such things as the sudden pounce of a cat, loud noises or the intrusion of rodents can cause fatal heart attacks as well as serious leg injuries. Preventive measures are especially important during the first few days after your pet's arrival home. New cages, toys, feeding devices and the cage wires should be carefully inspected for crevices or narrow holes or slots in which toes or toenails may become caught. Once a toe is trapped, the bird may struggle to free itself, twisting or injuring joints in the toes or legs. Depending on the severity of the experience, the bird may break a limb, suffer a bad sprain or even tear the tissue to the extent that a toe may wither and drop off later.

Broken leg: If there is a severe break with a dangling helpless limb, light splinting may be necessary, and it would be well to consult your veterinarian for help immediately. If no veterinarian is available, the broken limb should be aligned as carefully as possible, then gently and not too tightly wrapped with adhesive tape. Stretch the leg straight from the body by holding the toes and exerting gentle traction outward. Then use one-half inch adhesive tape, first around the area of the break and then in front, letting the edges stick together. Make several turns of the tape around the leg. Leave this on for approximately two weeks. If the break is in the thigh area, high up on the leg next to the body, pull the leg up into a sitting-leg position and tape it to the body. The leg should be healed in about two weeks.

Broken wing: Place the involved wing in its natural position next to the body. Take a short strip of one-quarter-inch adhesive tape and tape the wing-ends together at the rear of the body. After the wings are fixed, place a strip of adhesive tape around the wings and encompassing the body. Leave the tape on for approximately ten days.

To facilitate removal of the tape from legs or wings, use a bit of ether if it is available, acetone (nail polish remover) or any solvent recommended for removing tape from humans.

In caring for your canary when it is recovering from broken or dislocated bones, the most important precaution is to put it in a small cage without perches. Then place food and water on the floor of the cage where the bird can reach them without moving around.

Parasites: All birds, wild ones as well as cage birds, may become infested with parasites. Prevention is much more effective and pleasant than treatment for these pests. Careful attention to good housekeeping around singing and breeding cages will keep mites and lice away from your birds or will permit you to discover them early and take measures quickly. Parasites are divided into two classes: internal and external. Internal parasites such as *Coccidia* or worms are rarely found in canaries which are bred under controlled conditions. External parasites like mites and lice may bother your pet. Mites belong to the class Arachnida which includes spiders and scorpions. These creatures have eight legs—four on each side, and that is how you can distinguish them from lice. *Treatment:* Involves two stages. First you must kill the parasites on the bird and, at the same time, exterminate all mites in the cage. If you find mites on the canary, remove the bird from the cage and use one of the many good dusting powders that are available in pet shops. Apply the powder directly to the bird's body, especially under the wings. Work it well into the feathers.

At dawn, mites crawl off their victims and hide in nooks and crannies of the cage. They can be exterminated by one of several methods. Place the canary in a temporary cage. Now apply kerosene with a small brush to all places in the permanent cage where mites could lurk. Examine the perches and the perch ends particularly. Use one of the mite powders. Clean the cage with boiling water and then use a good disinfectant. Make sure the cage is thoroughly dry before returning the canary. Replace all perches with new ones.

The louse, which sometimes infests cage birds, is an insect with six legs. It feeds on the feathers instead of sucking the blood. Blowing a good insect powder into your pet's feathers with a small blower is the recommended method for getting rid of lice. Use the powder every four or five days for several weeks. Aerosol bird sprays have also proved highly effective in the prevention and eradication of these pests.

Above: Charcoal is thought to aid digestion, in birds as in people. Below: Oyster shells provide another source of calcium, which is particularly in demand during molting and egg laying.

44

Blue Border, a variety in which
melanin appears on a white ground.

A pair of canaries at the nest.

Above: Earthenware nestpans are the choice of some canary breeders; others recommend those made of metal or wire mesh. Below: Young canaries at the age at which they have just begun to eat on their own.

Breeding

Probably the most fascinating and creative aspect of canary keeping is breeding. Breeding is the key to shows and to social meetings with other canary fanciers. Most important of all, however, is the sense of creative achievement derived from this activity. Whether the beginner starts with one pair in a breeding cage or several pairs in a breeding aviary is immaterial—in either case both fun and possible profit are in the offing.

WHEN TO START

Many people believe that canary breeding should begin on St. Valentine's Day. Responsible pet shop experience suggests, however, that it is best to wait until March 1 or even March 25. This is especially true in particularly cold climates, even though your home is kept· at an even temperature.

Let's assume that you have a fine male and want to buy him a mate. Your best bet is to depend on a reputable dealer to select a good female of unrelated stock. Because genes are inherited from both parents, as much care should be used in selecting a female as is used in choosing a male. A male of excellent type mated to a poor-quality female is not likely to produce top-quality babies. It goes without saying that both parents should be of the same variety: in other words, Norwich should be bred to Norwich, Frill to Frill and so on.

Of course you will want to raise rich yellow, young birds, but don't make the mistake of trying to pair the two handsomest birds that you can find. The science of genetics is much too complex for a discussion here, but one point must be stressed. Colorful plumage is only one desirable characteristic. You also want fine singing, good carriage and, above all, healthy birds. Selecting mates on the basis of one trait only is not likely to pay off. Breeders have found, for example, that the correct mating is to pair a deep yellow male to a light yellow female. This will produce some youngsters with deep yellow plumage and some with feathers of a lighter yellow. The important point here, though, is that all the young birds will be healthy and handsome and have fine plumage.

THE BREEDING CAGE

The next step after selecting the birds is to provide a breeding cage. A simple, homemade cage will be satisfactory, but the commercially made cages available at pet shops are much better. The best size for the cage is 24 x 24 x 12 inches. These cages have both a solid and a wire partition in the center. The use of these partitions will be explained a little later when courtship is discussed. Of course, provide the necessary seed and water cups and make sure the perches are secure.

Next comes the nest. Metal nests are the easiest to clean and may be used over and over again. They can be bought from most pet shops, or your own can be made out of a kitchen soup strainer of suitable size. Remove the handle from the strainer and hang the nest about halfway down between the top of the cage and the floor. If you hang it too high, the parents will not be able to feed their youngsters. Remember, parent birds only feed their young when the young birds lift their heads and open their mouths, so they must be able to perch on the side of the nest with their heads just above the mouths of the babies.

COURTSHIP

Now that you have bought your pair of canaries and have prepared a breeding cage, you can look forward to having additions to the canary family. Suppose, however, you put the two birds in the cage and they appear to dislike each other or, even worse, have a tendency to fight! Here is where the commercial breeding cage comes in handy. Leave both partitions in the center of the cage. Put the male in one section and the female in the other. After four or five days, take out the solid partition so that the birds can see each other. When they are ready to mate, you will hear their mating call, and the male will feed the female through the bars. Then you can remove the remaining partition. It is almost certain that mating will soon take place.

You will know when to give the female nesting material because she will start picking up feathers and any soft stuff she can find in the cage. At this time, provide short pieces of soft string or cotton, dried moss and grass, or even nesting hair. *Caution:* Do not put long pieces of string in the cage. Your bird may use them for the nest and, sooner or later, the parents or young will get tangled up in them, perhaps fatally.

Breeding pairs should be disturbed as little as possible. When feeding the adults, it is advisable occasionally to peek into the nest, but disturbances should be kept to a minimum.

When the hen starts laying, she will lay one egg, usually very early in the morning, and another egg each successive

Above: The emerging feather sheaths are visible on these canary nestlings. Below: Nestlings exhibit the characteristic begging posture before their mother.

Facing page, above: The "double breeding cage" is so called because the enclosure can be partitioned into two compartments. Below: When feathers have developed to this stage, the youngsters are close to fledging.

Canary nestlings are fed by regurgitation. The swallowed food is temporarily held in the crop, a distensible portion of the esophagus. In this photograph, the food-filled crop is visible through the skin of the nestling's neck.

"Real" eggs kept in a nestpan outside the cage—their place in the nest inside is occupied by artifical ones.

day until three to six eggs have been laid. Replace each egg as it is laid with an artificial one, available from pet shops. Keep the eggs in a soft bed of absorbent cotton or soft cloth until the hen has laid her full number. Then remove the artificial eggs and return the real ones to the nest, and let her begin to incubate them. This procedure ensures that all the eggs will hatch at the same time. It is best for both the mother and for the fledglings if the babies are all born on the same day. This ensures uniformity of size. Otherwise the first baby to hatch would be much older and larger by the time the last egg had hatched. Incubation takes about two weeks.

EGG-BINDING

A mother bird will, on occasion, become egg-bound. The usual causes are insufficient exercise or the wrong diet. Get your birds in tip-top condition before breeding and you won't have this worry. The symptoms of egg-binding make the problem easy to diagnose. The hen will sit in obvious discomfort with her feathers puffed up. Later, her eyes will seem even more drawn and strained, and she will sit huddled on the floor. If you find a hen in this condition, you must act quickly.

Heat and mineral oil are the prescribed treatment. Place a drop or two of mineral oil directly into the bird's beak and the same amount into the vent. Be careful not to insert the dropper too deeply or you may break the egg. Make sure the oil is down to the point of the dropper in order not to force air into the bird. The heat may be supplied in several ways. Probably the best way is to wrap a hot-water bottle in a towel and place the suffering hen on the towel. The heat should be over 100°F. This temperature is very warm to the hand. Remember, the normal temperature of a canary is about 108°F.

SHOULD YOU LEAVE THE MALE IN THE CAGE?

Canary breeders are not in complete agreement about whether to remove the male from the cage while the hen is incubating the eggs. If you want the male to sing, transfer him to a song cage nearby. Some males may not sing at all when they are with their mate in the breeding cage. If the male is young and without experience in nesting, he may annoy the hen. In that case, you should remove him from the cage and place him in a cage nearby. If you have only one pair, it is probably best to leave the male with the hen so he can help raise the youngsters, so long as he seems to be helping rather than annoying her.

FEEDING YOUNG BIRDS

You do not have to do any of the work of feeding the young birds because the parents take care of it themselves.

You should provide egg food (in the form of biscuits, for example) and nestling food so that the parent birds will have suitable and nutritious food with which to feed their young. After the babies hatch, it will be about two and a half to three weeks before they leave the nest. After they leave the nest, the male parent continues to feed them for a while in response to the fluttering of their wings which indicates they are hungry. Young birds are voracious eaters and require feeding at very frequent intervals throughout the day. Make sure that the special food you furnish for the youngsters is on hand at all times.

Occasionally, parent birds neglect to feed their young. This usually happens when both parents are young birds raising their first family. For this reason, it is wise to have at least one parent about two years old, preferably the female. This is a good point to remember when you are selecting a mate for your first canary and plan to breed them for the first time. Your pet shop probably can sell you a hen who has raised at least one family. If the parents do not feed the young birds, the parent birds should be removed from the cage. You will have to take over the task by hand-feeding.

Moisten a combination of nestling food and egg biscuit and feed the baby birds from a small spatula. You probably won't have any difficulty in getting the babies to eat because the slightest movement over their nest will get them to open their mouths when they need food. At times it is possible to obtain a baby bird feeder in pet shops. This consists of two tubes, one fitted inside the other like a hypodermic syringe. The larger tube is filled with food, the smaller is then inserted as a plunger, and the food is slowly forced down the nestling's throat.

Canaries, like most songbirds, can raise more than one family in the breeding season. One of the problems for the beginning breeder is knowing when to remove the young from the first nest and knowing when to stop the breeding. Young birds can be taken away from their parents when they are five or six weeks old. Continue to feed the egg-biscuit and nestling food but also start to provide regular canary seed mixture. Young birds often have trouble handling hard seeds at first and may need some soft food for a time. For raising young canaries, many experts recommend egg food or egg-biscuit along with the nestling food. Remember, however, that hard seeds are the canary's natural food, and the babies should gradually be weaned to a seed diet. If they have trouble cracking the seeds, you can do it for them with a rolling pin—crack, don't crush.

THE LAST NEST

The question of when to allow the last nest is also of im-

Above: A Lizard chick being fed nestling food by hand. Below: In this instance, both parents cooperate in raising the youngsters.

Gloster Corona hen about to feed her brood.

A brood of recently fledged Yorkshires.

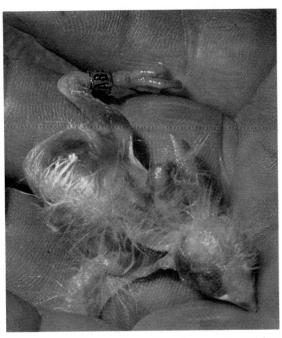

Above: Closed bands ensure positive identification. Banding must be done a few days after hatching; otherwise, the foot will be too large to accept the band. Below: Open bands are the only possibility for youngsters the size of these.

portance. Some beginners are so enthusiastic about the fine youngsters their pets are raising that they let the parents breed as long as they want to nest. When the birds are paired early, they could have three nests by the first of July. If the birds seem strong and healthy, the beginner is likely to permit one more nest. However, it is recommended that only one "clutch," or set of eggs, be permitted the first year. With more experience, you can then decide whether the birds can stand the rigors of a second or third clutch the following year.

Experience—with success as well as a few disappointments—is the only way to learn how to breed canaries successfully. Perhaps the biggest mistake any beginner can make is to become too interested in, too attentive toward his birds. Remember, birds want privacy in which to carry out their parental functions. Don't show off the nest, the first egg, the nestlings to every visitor. Give your pets a proper diet and privacy and they will do all the work. Provide help only when they need it.

MOLTING

Most birds, canaries among them, enter into molt soon after breeding. They should not be permitted to breed right up to the time they start molting. Molting, however, is a perfectly normal process and one that a healthy bird can go through with ease. It is not a good idea for them to molt while still raising their last brood. Give them a rest between the duties of a parent and the task of renewing their beautiful plumage for the coming year.

At about two months the young birds lose their body feathers during what is sometimes called the "baby molt." The flight feathers (the larger ones in the wings and tail) are not molted until the following season. Young birds that have gone through this baby molt are referred to as "unflighted birds." The following year, when all feathers have been molted and replaced, the birds are referred to as "flighted birds."

Adult canaries usually molt during the latter part of summer or the early part of fall. Warm climates trigger the molting season, causing it to begin earlier and to finish earlier. Cool climates delay the molt, causing it to last longer. In most areas, the molt will be completed in about six weeks. The usual regular care, keeping cages meticulously clean and keeping the birds out of drafts, will usually see them through the molt without problems. A commercially prepared molting food should be fed at this time to ensure a proper diet. Loss of feathers to such an extent that the canary shows bald spots or loses its ability to fly is abnormal and should be looked into. It may be because of poor diet, parasites or improper environment. (See the chapter entitled "Ailments and How to Treat Them.")

COLOR FEEDING

The topic of color feeding naturally follows a discussion of molting because such feeding must be done during the molting period. A great many novices don't know that birds bred for good natural color can have this color accentuated by feeding special food during the time of molting. Ask your pet dealer for "color food."

The exact time of the discovery that food could affect the color of a bird's plumage is not known—nor is the name of the discoverer. In the early days of color feeding, methods were kept secret by breeders, and there was much mystery about how the color was obtained. In fact, some of the early color-fed birds were disqualified from shows because the judges thought they had been dyed.

Apparently, cayenne pepper was the original ingredient used to produce color. A regular diet including a great deal of this pepper may appear a drastic measure to us, but the canaries seemed to suffer no ill effects. Nowadays most color food has carotenes as active ingredients. Also, some breeders are concerned that color feeding may cause liver damage.

Color feeding is a simple procedure using the commercially prepared color food that is available. First of all, it is wise to select birds of fine natural plumage that are ready for their second molt. Young birds can be color-fed, but the result is not uniform. As soon as the molt begins, feed color food every day without fail throughout the molting period. If you miss a day every now and then, the feathers will have washed-out spots and the bird will appear variegated. Some breeders feed a great deal of green food along with the color feeding because they feel that it helps set the color.

No color-fed bird should be allowed to remain in direct sunlight; its color will fade badly. It will retain its handsome appearance much longer if kept inside the house in an indirectly lighted room rather than in an outdoor aviary.

Above: During the period during which a bird is renewing its plumage (molting), its nutritional needs should receive special attention. Below: The tradition of color feeding continues in the Norwich fancy, even though today color receives many fewer points in the show standard than it once did.

Crested canary, showing the heavy feathering
which characterizes this breed.

Lancashire canary. In this "old variety,"
crested specimens are called "coppies."

Gloster Coronas—in showing Glosters, separate classes are set up for birds with crests and those without.

Showing Canaries

Many canary owners become so fascinated with these birds that they begin to breed canaries as a hobby. Once they have turned into really serious breeders, it is only a short step before they want to raise specimens for show and exhibit the outstanding canaries they have bred. Raising and training show canaries is an exacting but rewarding task.

For a beginning breeder, the first step toward learning all about your new hobby is to attend canary shows. At the shows you can learn about the many varieties of canaries and see them on the show bench. You will learn to tell the difference between a fine bird that is still only a beautiful pet and the show bird that wins prizes.

Probably the best way to get started is to become a member of an active bird club. Experienced club members are always willing to share their knowledge with new members. You can avoid many mistakes by accepting the advice that only an old hand can give.

Remember, a show specimen must be much more than a bird in perfect color and good health. A bird is judged on many other factors, including such things as size, depth of color, conformation and deportment. Particular attention is given to the bird's head, neck, shoulders, wings and so on. In addition to having a near-perfect bird, the exhibitor must train his birds so they do not flutter nervously or refuse to move correctly.

Your best canary may behave perfectly in the breeding rooms; it may accept the show cage readily. However, when you take it to its first formal show, the bird may flutter or fail to move promptly. If this should happen, the judge will refuse to consider the entry despite its other merits.

The solution to making show birds behave correctly is to train them carefully so you will be assured that they will be at their best when shown. First of all, they must become accustomed to the show cage by being frequently put into it. A small training stick about a foot long should be used to direct them from their regular cage into the show cage. Use this stick often so that when they see it they will know that you want them to move.

Show birds must become accustomed to strangers and be willing to let them handle the show cage, so while you are training your pets ask visitors to handle their cages quietly. In time, even nervous birds will learn to accept strangers.

As soon as you are convinced that you have birds capable of being shown, you should start their training. Since shows are usually held in the early fall when canaries are in their finest plumage, you will want to have your birds well trained before the announced date. Once you are sure your birds are well trained, you can reduce the training time, but continue to use the show cage throughout the show season.

GROOMING

All birds groom themselves and keep their feathers in top condition. Wild birds whose very life depends on the condition of their plumage spend hours every day in preening their feathers. This means that you do not have to worry too much about the bird's appearance because it will attend to it very well itself. In the first months after molting, a canary is at its best and will require little care. As the season wears on, however, the plumage may begin to show the effects of dirt and soot. Owners living in large industrial cities will be distressed to find their birds becoming dingier and dingier. In this situation, the only solution is to wash the birds.

Washing is a necessary evil in a sense since it is exhausting for the canary. Frequent washing, also, will affect the color and appearance of the plumage. It does, however, have to be done occasionally.

The best way to learn how to wash a bird is to have an experienced club member or pet shop employee demonstrate the procedure. The important points to remember are that the bird should be washed gently, rinsed thoroughly and dried carefully. The procedure should be carried out in a warm room absolutely free of drafts with a drying cage kept very warm until the bird is thoroughly dry.

Crooked and twisted feathers can usually be straightened by using hot water. Crests may sometimes lie raggedly after a wash and must be arranged into position.

In general, you will have to depend on careful breeding, good care, proper diet and the birds themselves in order to produce acceptable show specimens.

RECORD KEEPING

Keeping complete and accurate records is of vital importance to a breeder in any field. These records permit proper pairing and prevent matings that would weaken the stock. In a sense, these records are pedigrees since they permit the breeder to trace back the ancestry of each bird.

Above: Gloster Consort, a white nicely marked with blue. Below: Yellow Norwich hen, variegated. In this breed, the hard-texture feather ("yellow") looks as soft as the "buff" of other breeds.

Facing page:
The Border exhibited by Paul Dee won Third in the Type Canary division at the 1981 NIROC Show.

60

Border male, lightly variegated.

Above: Buff Cinnamon Yorkshire, variegated—"buff" refers to texture, "cinnamon" to the shade of color, and "variegated" to the presence of some area of dark feathering. Below: Buff Yorkshire, clear—"clear" indicates the absence of any dark feathering.

Records can be simple, but they should at least include the following information:

Good and bad points of each bird
Date of mating
Number of eggs laid
Number of birds hatched
Number of birds raised

Some of this information may appear unnecessary; however, it is useful in improving the stock. Neglectful parents or bad feeders and birds that seldom produce a good number of young birds must be weeded out of the breeding stock.

Once a sound breeding stock is established, the records will help the breeder to continue producing fine birds. They will let you advise others on how to pair birds they may purchase from you. When you want to buy additional birds, good records can assure you that your new birds are of unrelated stock and of the type you need.

SHOW SPECIMENS AND SOME STANDARDS

The most interesting show specimens are the type varieties, most of which were described earlier in this book. After a beginner has learned how to breed the commercial or pet canary, he is likely to branch out into the exciting field of type canaries. Here is a brief description of a perfect specimen of a type canary, in this case, the Yorkshire:

Form and position count for more points in the Yorkshire than in most other canaries. The bird should be about six and one-half inches long and must stand upright on long legs. Wing and tail feathers should be long and slender to impart the aristocratic shape necessary to win. Coloring, in general, is the same as with other canaries.

Here is a list of the points awarded to the perfect Yorkshire:

SCALE OF POINTS

Head 20
Body 10
Position 25
Condition 10
Size 10
Feather 25
                                                    Total: 100

Position, obviously, is one of the two most important factors in gaining points for the Yorkshire. This fact makes the training of these canaries especially important because nervous birds will be destined for defeat.

TRAINING

Training of the bird should begin at an early age: when it is about four weeks old. At that time, a show cage should be hung in the aviary and the young bird introduced to it so that it will become used to being on display and attracting public attention. It is wise to let visitors gently handle the bird under the breeder's supervision so that natural habits of relaxation will be formed. The use of the training stick has already been described. Here let it be repeated that this implement should be used *gently* as a *guide* toward proper movement, not as an instrument of compulsion. Use it to induce the young birds to run into the show cage frequently so they may be managed easily when the real competition starts.

In about two weeks, the young birds should be conditioned to the show cage and emphasis on position training can then begin. Since, occasionally, birds tend to slouch so that they do not reach the required position (60 degrees by British standards for Yorkshires), it is necessary to train them in erectness. A simple technique is to place a number of birds in several cages side by side. Put a dividing barrier of cardboard cut to the proper height between the cages so that the canaries will have to stretch upward in order to see each other. Results should be apparent within a week.

The Border presents a slightly different training problem. Its position should be the same as that of the Yorkshire but, when running the perches, it tends to drop to an angle of 45 degrees. This 15-degree loss can be corrected by encouraging the canaries to travel the perches in a jaunty manner. Move one hand across the outside of the cage slightly higher than the birds' heads. As they follow, heads erect to watch the movement, sweep the other hand back from the opposite side. The continuous motion will instill proper habits of erect traveling in the young birds. This method is also applicable to the Gloster.

SHOW TIPS

One of the problems confronting the new canary hobbyist who seeks to enter the show world is the tendency to aim too high. It is usually wiser for the tyro breeder to enter the less competitive local shows until he has acquired a fine polish of experience.

One of the best reasons for initial concentration on local events lies in the difficulty inherent in packing and shipping canaries to distant shows. Transportation agents cannot be relied upon to feed and water the birds and not infrequently the pets are left for hours in exposed areas or placed next to cats or dogs. The result is a sick or upset bird unfit for show competition.

If birds must be shipped to distant shows, they should go Air Express prepaid. An over-ration of seed and water should be placed in the box or cage. Do not place paper on the cage or cage bottom because the seed could be strewn

Dilute blue and dilute fawn Border canaries. The "ideals" depicted by R. A. Vowles are still current today.

Award-winning Cinnamon Border in the standard show cage.

Border canary. In this breed, good conformation is a
matter of curves running smoothly into one another.

there and, if it gets underneath the paper, the bird will starve. A small sponge placed in the water cup will reduce water loss due to splashing.

Not too infrequently the show-oriented hobbyist will find himself in a position where he may be asked to take part in the management of a show. The roles here are many and varied, ranging anywhere from stewardship and public relations to actual judging and secretarial work.

Show personnel should be selected as many months in advance as possible. A good show is the result of good teamwork; the sooner the members of the team start working together, the better the show will be.

Small shows do have their problems. Less soundly financed, they frequently cause a drain on the pocketbooks of those taking part. However, they are such a boon to the beginning breeder that any financial loss is offset by the experience gained.

Gloster Corona. At many shows the number of Gloster entries is exceeded only by the number of Borders, which testifies to the growing popularity of this recently developed breed.

General Tips

White Yorkshire with blue eye-and-wing markings.

As can readily be seen, the canary hobby is one capable of infinite expansion. Though in its elementary stages it can be a source of enjoyment to almost everyone, in its advanced stages it enters into the realm of Big Business, and a much more scientific approach is necessary. Here, again, it might be appropriate to include some additional details on a few aspects touched on lightly earlier.

There are certain principles which should be followed unconditionally, especially where the breeding house or home aviary are concerned. These are proper ventilation, an absence of drafts, a complete lack of dampness, an absence of pests and insects (particularly rats), a steady level of temperature and good but not excessive lighting.

In brief, it should be pointed out that drafts, dampness and abrupt fluctuations in temperature are the cause of the majority of bird fatalities. Rats are a constant danger to birds housed in an outdoor aviary. More than one breeder has reported that despite the best of precautions rats have gotten to his stock, resulting in irreplaceable loss.

Another aspect of the canary-keeping hobby that some "aficionados" find of interest is building their own cages. Many breeders prefer to do this because of their special requirements or because they have an aptitude with tools. Actually, the dollar saving is minimal, since one must not only purchase materials, but he must also invest his own time and effort.

Many breeders like to build their own canary flight in some convenient corner of the breeding room. This consists of an area six feet high, six feet long and four feet wide, screened with half-inch wire mesh. This will give young birds confined to breeding cages an opportunity to get more exercise and build up their health.

VACATION CARE

One of the most important things that a canary fancier who plans on taking a vacation or business trip can do is to place his pet in the care of a pet shop furnishing boarding service. There the pet will receive experienced care and will not be subject to possible accidents or improper care by an inexperienced friend or neighbor. In most cases, the fee is nominal. Some pet shops even offer a "visiting service" for the breeder whose stock requires attention while he is away.

Facing page: Color-fed Norwich male.

Border canaries, clear and variegated.

SUMMER CARE

Canaries, generally, should be kept in a room temperature of approximately 70°F. and should be fed once daily. During excessively hot weather, give the bird fresh, cool water several times a day. A cloth dampened in cold water may be placed around three sides of the cage to serve as a refresher. Above all, keep the pet away from air conditioners and drafts. Both can be fatal.

HOLDING A CANARY

You will have had your first lesson in how to handle a canary by remembering how the bird was caught and transferred to your cage when you purchased it. The usual way is to hold the bird in the palm of your hand with fingers gently encircling the body. The hand is brought down on the back of the bird in such a way that the wings can be gently folded in natural position. You will soon learn how to do this so that the bird cannot escape, but it still is not so tightly held as to cause panic or prevent normal breathing. It will be easier to catch the bird (and with less chance of injury) if perches and toys are removed temporarily.

CATCHING AN ESCAPED BIRD

If your bird escapes from the cage, first of all move slowly so that you don't frighten your canary into wild flight. Look around the room and make sure that doors are closed, electric fans are turned off and any other hazards such as open flames or cooking vessels are properly tended. Now you are ready to catch your little pet. If it is nighttime you can wait until your bird stops flying and then turn off the lights. When your eyes are accustomed to the darkness and you can see the bird, it is a simple matter to catch it since it will perch quietly in the dark.

Generally speaking, however, canaries are not difficult to catch even in the light. Above all don't rush about madly; merely walk slowly around until you have the bird cornered. If you have rooms with high ceilings or have difficulty in moving around yourself, you may want to purchase a long-handled catching net of the type used in pet stores.

If you have time or don't want to chase after the bird, you can leave the cage door open and your bird will eventually return to the cage for food and water.

Some bird owners keep a perching stick or dowel three to five feet in length handy and use it to recover canaries from high places. The stick is slowly brought in front of the bird so that it can hop onto the stick and then be carried back to the cage. A little patience is needed until your pet learns to trust you and the stick.

Above: Catching and holding a canary is occasionally necessary for health inspection, trimming claws, and so forth. Below: Gloster Corona—established in this century, Glosters have become one of the most popular types for breeding and exhibiting.

Two Red-factors and a Lizard.

Combining mutations has produced many subtle colors, such as the Silver Agate above and the Blue Opal below.

Training to Perform Tricks

BIRD BRAINS

Many bird lovers have found themselves the unfortunate butt of humor regarding the intelligence of their pets. "Bird-brained" is a disparaging term which has come to be synonymous with stupidity. It is grossly unfair to the birds.

Researchers now know that the intelligence and mental adaptability of birds—and this includes canaries—far exceeds that of some other animals. The confusion is a result of the common practice of considering memory and intelligence as the same. Although memory is an element of intelligence, the capacity to reason and adapt does not depend exclusively on conscious recall. Here is where the bird is more efficient than—if not superior to—the mammal; it relies on an instinctual, unconscious memory (a memory constituted of habit) rather than on a conscious and synthetic one.

Because of this ability to learn, canaries are frequently studied in animal behavior laboratories. Training is accomplished through a system of rewards and punishments. Food to a hungry canary is an adequate reward.

TRICK TRAINING

You will notice that everyday your little bird will become more tame as it comes to know and trust you. Tricks are more difficult and will require a great deal of patience, understanding and imagination on your part.

Let's consider some of the simpler tricks which you can teach your bird. First, remove all perches and feeding vessels from the cage and hold a short perch, pencil or your outstretched index finger in the cage. With patience and perseverance, you can entice your bird to perch without fear. Try this approach every day but only for short periods of time. Move your hand slowly and keep the rest of your body as motionless as possible. Remember that birds have a natural fear of movements overhead, so keep the cage at eye level. If the cage is on a table, you will be less frightening to your bird if you are seated quietly by the cage, while your hand moves slowly in the cage.

With patience you will find that your canary will eat seeds or other tidbits from your fingers or from the palm or back of your hand.

Facing page: A pair of Border canaries.

The following are some general guidelines of training which make for entertaining home shows:

Start the training early, while the bird is still a nestling. Finger-train it first; then teach it more advanced tricks.

A trained canary requires more food than does an untrained one. Use the treat-reward system to inspire it and keep it up to a high standard.

Birds are extremely sensitive and go into shock easily since their heart rate is so great. Therefore, never frighten the bird by losing your temper.

Start your training in trios and pairs of birds so they will be company for each other.

Once you have accustomed your birds to finger perching, obtain a small perching bar eight or ten inches long and, working seated at a small table, bring the bar gently across the birds' chests so they will hop on to it. Then reverse the procedure so they will hop from bar to finger. The second stage is to place the bar slightly higher than their beaks so they will fly to it and then back to the finger.

Do not train the canaries more than a half hour per day; a longer period is exhausting. After about a week, advance them to shoulder perching and stair climbing, the stairs consisting of a staggered row of thin books.

The next training phase requires a 24-inch training stick one-quarter-inch in diameter. Tap it lightly on the table top about two inches behind their tail feathers. On either side of the birds, place a row of books six inches apart. Giving the verbal command, "Forward march," *gently* advance the stick until the birds move forward and back in military formation. Eventually, the stick may be discarded and the birds will drill on verbal command alone.

Changing positioning of the books permits the birds to be guided into various types of drill formations such as various circular and linear patterns. Also, substitution of other objects (apples, oranges, bookends or decorative vases for example) for the books tend to heighten the dramatic effect.

Another way of using books is to open them and place them lengthwise on the training table so that they offer a "tunnel" effect. The birds may be trained to walk through the tunnel and then fly to the top of the book and perch there.

A circular basket can be placed on its side and several birds perched on its top. As the basket rolls gently from side to side, the pets will perform a natural balancing act.

The following rules *must* be strictly adhered to:

Never force a bird through an act; if it refuses, put it back in the cage and resume training the next day.

Always reward the canary with a treat afterward.

The color achieved here is called Frosted Green Agate Pastel.

A group of Border Canaries.

Frosted Rose Isabel.

A tired bird cannot learn. Don't set too high a standard.

Visit your retailer and look for little plastic toys such as ferris wheels, merry-go-rounds or other light moving toys such as cars or baby carriages. These toys have places in which seeds or other foods may be placed, and when your canary eats, the pecking will cause the toys to move. Again patience is required while the bird learns to trust these new objects. There are even tiny plastic scales on which your bird can weigh itself while eating its seeds.

We have talked about love, patience and the food reward and made a few suggestions for the use of trick toys. Now is the time to start using your imagination to see what other tricks you can think of. Try placing three light sewing thimbles in the cage and fill them with seed. When your canary is used to these objects and eats readily from them, turn the thimbles upside down with a few seeds under each. Allow a few seeds to stick out under the edges of the thimbles. When it has learned to turn the thimbles over to get to the seed you are ready to try the old "shell game," so familiar in carnivals. That is, you can put seeds under one of the three thimbles and your canary will tip over thimbles to find the seed.

Just how far you go in training your canary will depend upon your imagination and patience. We have talked about training merely to indicate that canaries can be trained if you wish to spend the time and effort. If not, there is nothing lost, because you still have the pleasure of listening to the beautiful song.